WORLD
SUPER CARRIERS

Osprey Colour Series

**Tony Holmes and
Jean-Pierre Montbazet**

WORLD
SUPER CARRIERS

Naval air power today

Published in 1988 by Osprey Publishing Limited
27A Floral Street, London WC2E 9DP
Member company of the George Philip Group

British Library Cataloguing in Publication Data

Holmes, Tony
    World super carriers: naval air power today.
    1. France. Marine. Aircraft carriers
    2. United States. Navy. Aircraft carriers
    I. Title   II. Montbazet, Jean-Pierre
    628.8′255′0944

ISBN 0–85045–848–X

Editor Dennis Baldry
Captions by Mike Jerram
Designed by Norman Brownsword
Printed in Hong Kong

Title pages A flight deck officer from USS *John F Kennedy* caught in balletic pose amid catapult steam as he motions to the crew of a Lockheed S-3A Viking anti-submarine warfare aircraft from squadron VS-22

Right Scene from the hangar deck of the USS *John F Kennedy* as weak sunlight breaks through to brighten the white-capped ocean

Right A-7E Corsair of VA-97 'War Hawks' spotted in the tie-down area on the deck of CVN-70 USS *Carl Vinson* in 1986. The *Vinson's* A-7 attack squadrons have since re-equipped with McDonnell Douglas F/A-18 Hornets

Contents

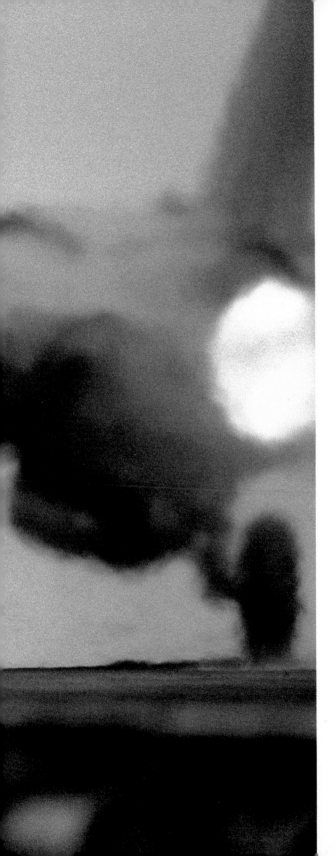

Terminator

This page and overleaf Afterburner! Riding 40,000 lbs thrust from its two Pratt & Whitney TF30-P-412A turbofan engines, F-14A Tomcat side number 212 of VF-32 'Swordsmen' blasts off from one of the USS *John F Kennedy's* waist catapults. Note marked (but not full) upward deflection of all-moving tailplane as the catapult shot begins, and differential action as the Tomcat climbs away

9

White heat from the afterburner of a VF-14 'Tophatters' sears the jet blast deflector (JBD) on the deck of USS *John F Kennedy* at the start of a night cat shot. Glowing green strips on the nose, wingtips and aft section are 'tape light' panels to aid station keeping on night formation flying

Night bolter. Deck landing is a heart-quickening business at the best of times, but night traps are when carrier pilots really earn their flight pay. Here a Tomcat misses the wire (note the sparks from the arrestor hook striking the deck) and 'bolters' for another try

F-14A Tomcat from VF-1, 'Wolfpack', still retaining high visibility stars 'n' bars and stencil marks awaits a cat shot on the USS *Ranger*. VF-1 was the first operational squadron to receive Tomcats, commissioning at NAS Miramar, California on 14 October 1972

Tomcat driver from VF-14 'Tophatters' aboard
USS *John F Kennedy*

Tomcat's snout. Note muzzle of the General
Electric M61A1 Vulcan 20 mm gun in port side,
and chin-mounted Northrop Television Camera
Sight (TCS) which can scan a 30 degree field of
view, tracking targets even under high G
conditions and giving the backseat Radar
Intercept Officer (RIO) a magnified image of the
'bogey' for identification. The Hughes AN/AWG-9
radar can simultaneously track up to 24 targets
and attack six of them, and is capable of
detecting fighter-sized aircraft at ranges up to
195 miles

These pages The 'Swordsmen' from VF-32 were among the first US Navy Atlantic Fleet squadrons to become operational on Tomcats. With VF-14's 'Tophatters' they achieved a 100 per cent kill rate during missile firing exercises on their first Mediterranean cruise aboard the USS *John F Kennedy* in 1975, but this sequence of a 'Swordsmen' Tomcat shooting the bow cat from *JFK* dates from 1986. The F-14A is launched in the 'kneeling' position with the nosewheel strut compressed. As the catapult completes its stroke the energy in the compressed strut is released, pitching the nose of the aircraft up into the correct flying attitude

Step aboard, but better ask the CAG first. This is the Commander Air Wing's personal F-14A from VF-213 'Black Lions' aboard the USS *Enterprise*

A 'Fighting Aardvarks' F-14A from VF-114 aboard USS *Enterprise*. Note AIM-9M Sidewinder air-to-air missile mounted on the starboard outboard wing glove stores station

What big teeth you have. VF-1 'Wolfpack' F-14A aboard USS *Ranger*

Open gun and magazine bays display the Tomcat's six-barrel General Electric M61A1 Vulcan rotary cannon and ammunition drum for 675 rounds of 20 mm. To avoid the possibility of spent ammunition cases being ingested into the Tomcat's large engine intakes, here protected with what appear to be makeshift covers of camouflage material, empty cases are returned to the drum after being extracted from the gun breech

Main picture **The 'Swordsmen' of VF-32 have retained some of the bright heraldry, despite the move towards toned-down low visibility markings on US Navy carrier aircraft in recent years**

Inset **A Sidewinder and Sparrow-armed Tomcat of VF-213 'Black Lions' about to trap aboard the USS** *Enterprise*. **Piles of yellow wheel chocks in the foreground**

Left Tomcat in a trap. The target wire is number three of four. Aiming for the early wires can be hazardous if the aircraft gets too low, risking a deck strike; too high, even by a foot, and it's a bolter—a go around for another pass. This F-14 has just been brought to the usual violent, harness jerking halt by the arrestor cable. Note the nosewheel leg fully compressed by deceleration, the extended dorsal airbrake and smoke from the engines as the pilot anticipates the 'trap' and pushes the throttles to military power in case of a bolter

Below 'Tophatter' trails his hook along JFK's deck

These pages Even on the big CVN supercarriers deck space is always at a premium with 90 aircraft aboard. 'Spotting' the aircraft, particularly during flying operations, demands the skills of a champion jigsaw puzzlist, though interlocking Tomcats—seen here aboard the USS *John F Kennedy*—is made easier by an oversweep feature which enables its variable-geometry wings to be swept to 75 degrees, overlapping the tailplanes. Maximum inflight sweep is 68 degrees

Hornet interlude

Left VFA-131's 'Wildcats' also took part in the Libyan raids. One of their F/A-18s is seen here aboard *Coral Sea* with Grumman A-6Es from VA-55 'Warhorses' in foreground. The 'Wildcats' were the first Atlantic Fleet squadron to become operational with the Hornet

Below Hornet's sting? No, just the retractable inflight refuelling probe of a McDonnell Douglas F/A-18 Hornet. Unlike the USAF, which uses boom/receptacle flight refuelling, the US Navy favours the hose-drogue method which enables non-dedicated aircraft such as A-6s and A-7s to serve as tankers using 'buddy' refuelling packs

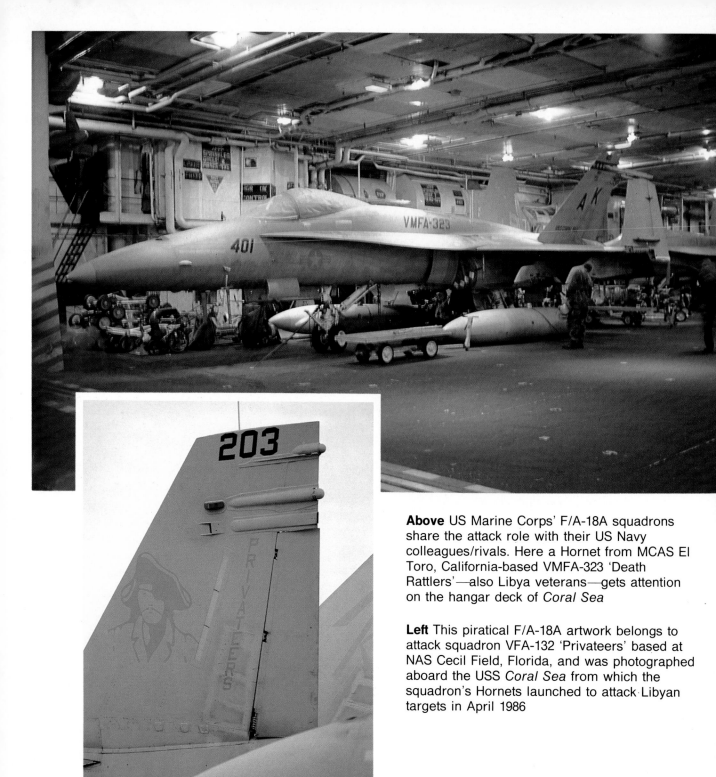

Above US Marine Corps' F/A-18A squadrons share the attack role with their US Navy colleagues/rivals. Here a Hornet from MCAS El Toro, California-based VMFA-323 'Death Rattlers'—also Libya veterans—gets attention on the hangar deck of *Coral Sea*

Left This piratical F/A-18A artwork belongs to attack squadron VFA-132 'Privateers' based at NAS Cecil Field, Florida, and was photographed aboard the USS *Coral Sea* from which the squadron's Hornets launched to attack Libyan targets in April 1986

Above A red-shirted ordnance man checks the wingtip AIM-9 Sidewinder station of a 'Privateers' Hornet aboard the USS *Coral Sea*

Overleaf Replenishment at (Coral) Sea. The big nuclear carriers come with several years of fuel, but older oil-burning ships such as *Coral Sea* must rendezvous with a fueller to 'top up' or RAS. Regular ship-to-ship transfusions of jet fuel for the JP-5 guzzling Air Wings are needed by all carriers. Note ordnance multiple ejector racks (MERs) stored in the 'pit' to right

These pages A quiet moment for deck crewmen aboard *Coral Sea* amid parked Hornets from the two US Navy and two Marine Corps squadrons detached to the carrier. The F/A-18 performs the same air-to-air/air-to-ground roles for the US Navy as the General Dynamics F-16 does for the USAF, only better Navy aviators would claim. As a fighter its Hughes AN/APG-65 multi-mode digital tracking radar can track ten targets simultaneously, displaying eight to the pilot. Air

air weapons for the Hornet include AIM-7
Sparrow, AIM-9 Sidewinder and AIM-120
AMRAAM missiles, while for surface attack the
aircraft can carry AGM-65 Mavericks with a
Martin Marietta AN/ASQ-173 laser spot
tracker/strike camera and Ford AN/AAS-38 FLIR
pod replacing Sparrows on the fuselage nacelle
stores stations. AGM-84 Harpoon anti-ship
missiles are also in the Hornet's weapons
inventory

Left A brown-shirted plane captain puts some elbow grease into the cockpit area of a USMC VMFA-314 'Black Knights' Hornet aboard USS *Coral Sea*. Those big navy-issue boots are great for foot protection but . . . they leave their mark on the lift-generating Leading Edge Extension (LEX) strakes of the F/A-18A. Current dull finish low visibility paint and toned down markings of US Navy aircraft are unpopular with pilots and decks crews alike, lacking the panache of the old semi-gloss light gull grey and white colour scheme, whilst being more prone to heavy weathering and much more difficult to keep *looking* clean, even when it is spotless. That is, of course, all part of the camouflage experts' plan

Above Stinging Hornet? Yes, indeed. This F/A-18A aboard the USS *Constellation* is from VFA-113 'Stingers', who must bemoan the passing of high visibility colours when their bee insignia was more strikingly marked on A-7Es in black, yellow and red. Huge trailing edge flaps of the Hornet are at maximum 45 degree droop

'MiniWACS'

Left Yellowshirt FDO supervises deck parking of a Grumman E-2C Hawkeye from VAW-126 aboard the USS *John F Kennedy*

Overleaf A 'mule' tow tractor hauls an E-2C Hawkeye to its parking spot on the USS *Coral Sea*. The Hawkeye's 2000 lb (910 kg) Randtron AN/APA-171 rotodome, colloquially known as the frisbee, measures 24 feet (7.3 metres) in diameter and is seen here lowered to the fully stowed position to enable it to fit into carrier hangar decks. Huge Hamilton Standard propellers are of mixed steel and foam/glassfibre construction, Driven by a pair of 4910 shp (3661 kW) Allison T56-A-425 turboprop engines. Along with their C-2A Greyhound carrier-on-board delivery counterparts and a few remaining Grumman C-1A Traders, the Hawkeyes are the only propeller-driven aircraft still operating aboard US Navy carriers. E-2Cs have been exported to Egypt, Israel, Japan and Singapore

These pages and overleaf Despite its size, the E-2C's maximum takeoff weight is less than that of a stores-laden A-6E or a 'clean' F-14A, and poses no problem for the catapult. Plane Guard SAR SH-3 helicopters aside, 'Hummers' are invariably the first aircraft to launch during flying operations and the last to recover. Their role is to provide the carrier battle group with over-the-horizon airborne early warning surveillance. The Hawkeye 'MiniWACS'' AN/APS-125 search radar (AN/APS-138 on post-1983 production, and steadily being retrofitted throughout the fleet) can detect targets as small as a cruise missile up to 155 nm miles away, fighters at 200 nm or more, and can track as many as 250 targets simultaneously. The Hawkeye can also act as a 'memory' dump for the carrier's CAP F-14As' AWG-9 radars, storing a Tomcat's 24 targets in its memory bank while the fighter is freed to acquire a further two dozen. Fuel and weapon status of F-14As can also be up- or downlinked to the E-2C's computers, enabling the Hawkeye's 'moles'—the air controller, combat information officer and radar operator who work in the dark confines of its fuselage—to deploy their forces most effectively. A typical Carrier Air Wing has a detachment of four E-2Cs. This VAW-126 example is operating from the USS *John F Kennedy*

It is not known at the time of writing whether the portly COD C-2s will succumb to the march of low visibility markings in the US military. Hopefully, the doubly in-aptly named Greyhound will continue to add a welcome splash of colour aboard American carriers. This example has just arrived on *JFK*

Above This little piggy . . . Orange razorback insignia on this sunset splashed E-2C identifies it as the property of VAW-114, 'Hormel Hogs'. Though not visible here, VAW-114 usually have a litter of tiny porkers running around the circumference of their rotodomes

Intruding

A heavily weather-worn A-6E TRAM
Intruder of VA-75 'Sunday Punchers' halts on
John F Kennedy's catapult track to wait for the
shuttle's return

Above Greenshirt maintenance men attend to a 'Sunday Punchers' Intruder's capacious radome bay. The hemispherical fairing below the A-6E's nose houses TRAM (Target Recognition And Attack, Multisensor) equipment comprising FLIR, a laser rangfinder and tracker, and spot designator in a radar integrated, stabilized turret

Right Already hitched up to their 'mules', A-6Es wait to be towed out for launch aboard JFK

Right Intruders, a Prowler and an interloping Tomcat on *John F Kennedy's* deck. The blue/grey low-viz Intruders are US Marine Corps aircraft from VMA(AW)-533 'Hawks', while the grey/white VA-75 machine in the foreground is a KA-6D dedicated tanker variant, identified by the fairing for the hose/drogue deployment system below the word 'Navy'

Above Marine Corps' 'Hawks' A-6E TRAM on JFK's side elevator. Six USMC squadrons fly the A-6

High-viz, low-viz. Contrasting tails of US Navy
and US Marine Corps KA-6D and A-6E on JFK's
hangar deck

truders from the 'Sunday Punchers' and
awks' share JFK deck space with a Douglas
A-3B Skywarrior 'Whale' electronic intelligence
thering (ELINT) aircraft detached from its base
Rota, Spain

Left **With emergency procedures checklist and his 35 mm SLR camera stowed on the glareshield, this A-6E bombardier/navigator prepares to launch from JFK**

Below left **All thumbs. Flight deck officer and greenshirts give it the** *Go!* **signal**

Main picture **Fly 1 beckons A-6E TRAM side number 505 onto the cat track**

A USMC 'Hawks' A-6E, nose gear strut extended, waits for the catapult shuttles tug which will accelerate it from zero . . .

. . . to 150 knots in an instant. Greenshirts look nonchalant as the Intruder goes off the *John F Kennedy's* waist cat

Above Gear down, hook down, flaps down, slats out, airbrakes extended, a VMA(AW)-533 A-6E TRAM looks for the third wire aboard JFK. This aircraft is carrying a Sargent-Fletcher D704 'buddy' inflight refuelling pack on its centreline stores station

Right In the groove. This A-6E TRAM is perfectly aligned for a textbook 'trap' aboard *John F Kennedy*. Note the Intruder's fully open split wingtip speedbrakes, adopted after trials with the Grumman A2F-1 prototype showed that rear fuselage dive brakes disrupted airflow over the tail surfaces. Each carrier squadron has a Landing Signal Officer (LSO), an experienced pilot who monitors and grades every 'trap' made by his colleagues. There are four grades: *OK* (the naval aviator's way of saying excellent); *Fair*, not good, but safe; *No grade*, dangerous to pilot, other crewmen and aircraft; and *Cut*, so unsafe that a crash could easily have occurred

Left The stabilizer mechanism from an A-6E of VA-145 'Swordsmen' shore-based at NAS Whidbey Island, Washington, gets attention aboard the USS *Ranger*

Above Close parking aboard *Ranger*—A-6E TRAM of US Marine Corps squadron VMA(AW)-121 'Green Knights'

Above Grumman EA-6B Prowler is a four-seat
electronic warfare development of the Intruder,
built around the AN/ALQ-99F tactical jamming
system. This Prowler from VAQ-134 'Garudas'
on the side lift of USS *Carl Vinson* displays the
gold plated canopies adopted as an
(unnecessary, as it transpired) crew protection
measure against microwave emissions from the
ECM equipment

Top right The EA-6B's jamming system is
housed in up to five external pods, three of
which are carried by this example from VAQ-136
'Gauntlets' embarked aboard USS *Midway*, but
seen here at NAS Atsugi, Japan. A total of ten
jamming transmitters can be carried, each pod

covering up to seven frequency bands with
simultaneous jamming in any two on ICAP-2
(increased capability) versions of the Prowler.
The large fin tip pod houses sensitive
surveillance receivers for long range detection
of radars

Right EA-6B poised for the cat shot aboard USS
Ranger. This Prowler carries two jamming pods
and two 300 US gallon (1135 litre) drop tanks.
Tiny propellers on the ECM pods windmill in
flight to provide power via a Garrett AiResearch
ram-air turbine. The radiation symbol on the
EA-6B's nose helps Landing Signal Officers
differentiate Prowlers from Intruders when
viewed head-on during landing approaches

The French Way

This page and overleaf France and the Phillippines were the only countries outside the USA to operate the elegant Crusader. Forty-two were delivered to the *Aéronavale* from 1964 onwards, and—retrofitted with F-8J standard wings for extended fatigue life and some with new afterburners for their Pratt & Whitney J57-PW-20 engines—26 survive, 14 of them serving with 12F at Landivisiau. Crusaders are due to disappear from French service by 1995, replaced by the new *Avion de Combat Marine*, based on a 'navalized' version of the AMD Rafale B. *Foch*, on which all pictures in this chapter were shot, is one of two French carriers (the other is *Clemenceau*), and was launched in 1963. *Foch* and *Clemenceau* will also retire by the end of the next dacade, to be replaced by the Ports Aéronefs Nucléaire (PANs—nuclear aircraft carriers) *Charles de Gaulle* and *Richelieu*

Above *Quel canard!* Belligerent Donald Duck is
the squadron emblem of France's *Aéronautique
Navale Flotille 12*, which flies Vought F-8E(FN)
Crusaders. Here a 12F pilot gets settled in his
bang seat prior to launch from the 32,780 ton
carrier *Foch*

These pages 'Blousons bleu'—blue jackets—
prepare an F-8E(FN) for launch from *Foch*.
French Navy Crusaders can carry two Matra
R.530 radar guided missiles, modified for
compatibility with their AN/APQ-104 radar, or
four Matra R.550 Magic or AIM-9 Sidewinder
AAMs. This one totes a pair of Magics on its
fuselage stations. Note Westland Lynx HAS Mk
2(FN) hovering on plane guard duty abeam the
carrier

Foch and the Crusader still use the old hook
and bridle method of catapult launching

Thanks to its tilting wing, the Crusader's incidence can be increased to enhance lift during take off and landing whilst permitting the fuselage to remain in a near level attitude for good pilot vision

Above *Non*, he hasn't damaged his nosewheel. Castoring gear is useful for manoeuvring on deck and into tight parking spots. Note twin 20 mm cannon ports

Right AMD Super Etendards and a Breguet Alize ASW aircraft ranged beneath *Foch's* bridge, watched over by the flyco in his glazed cab

Above Dating from 1964, this Dassault Etendard IVP tactical reconnaissance aircraft is one of 12 survivors from 22 built and four others converted from IVMs, and is operated by 16F from Landivisiau. Like *Aéronavale* Crusaders, Etendard IVPs took part in raids on the Lebanon in 1983. This one is finished in the two-tone blue/grey disruptive camouflage scheme progressively adopted on Etendards since 1984

Standard bearer. Super Etendard pilot mounts his steed for another mission from *Foch*. Nose radome houses a Thompson-CSF Agave radar which provides air-to-surface and air-to-air search modes and target designation for long range active homing missiles such as Exocet, used to devastating effect by Argentinian Super Etendards against British shipping in the Falklands War. Air-to-air range is between 11–17 miles (18–28 kilometres), and more than 60 miles (96 kilometres) in air-to-surface mode against a destroyer-size target. ESD Anemone track-while-scan radar and improved avionics will be fitted in a planned upgrade programme beginning in 1991

Deck crew attach the catapult bridle prior to launching a Super Etendard, 71 of which were built for the *Aeronvale*. They operate with 11F and 14F at Landivisiau and 17F at Hyeres

Above Catapult steam swirling around the double-slotted flaps and excellent forward vision from the cockpit are evident as the Super Etendard starts its brief journey along the *Foch's* catapult track

Right Although this example carries only a pair of 1100 litre (290 US gallon) drop tanks, the Super Etendard can carry Matra Magic AAMs, an AM39 Exocet anti-ship missile, 60 mm rocket pods, up to 27 BAP 100 or BAT 120 bombs, or the AN52 nuclear bomb. Conversion of 53 Super Etendards to carry the Aérospatiale ASMP stand-off nuclear weapon was proceeding in early 1988

This page and overleaf **Textbook traps aboard** *Foch* **for 17F Super Etendards**

Allons-Y! Foch's **Deck handlers tow Super Etendards out at the start of the day's flying operations while the crew of the plane guard Lynx helo wait for their call to duty**

A Super Etendard is towed out at the start of the day's flying

Eighteen Alouette IIIs are on the strength of
Servitude squadrons 22S and 23S at lanvéoc
and St Mandrier, for training, liaison, search-
and-rescue and (as here) carrier plane guard
duty

Super Etendards and a sole F-8E(FN) Crusader
spotted on *Foch's* stern deck parking areas

Up she rises: Breguet Alizé on *Foch's* side lift

These pages and overleaf The Alizé is surely among the oldest aircraft still serving with the naval air arm of any major power (and one of very few propeller driven types still flying off carriers), having first been delivered to the Aéronavale in 1959. Powered by two Rolls-Royce Dart turboprops turning contra-rotating propellers, the Alizé is an anti-submarine patrol aircraft with limited attack capability using Aérospatiale AS.12 anti-ship missiles, and also performs SAR duties. Twenty-eight Alizés, including these detached to *Foch* from 6F at Nimes-Garons, have been updated to *Nouvelle Generation* configuration with new communications and navigation equipment, Thomson-CSF Iguane radar in the ventral retractable 'dustbin' and passive ECM in the noses of the underwing landing gear pods. A small number of Alizés also remain on the strength of the Indian Navy, the only other operator of the type

V/STOL

Harrier swansong. US Marines Corp's squadron VMA-513 was first to receive Hawker AV-8A Harriers in April 1976. Ten years later, flying the same aircraft upgraded to AV-8C standard with avionics updates, ECM gear, provision for triple ejector racks (TERs) on outer pylons and ventral strake lift improvement devices (LIDs), VMA-513 undertook their last operational deployment with the early Harrier before transitioning to the much more capable McDonnell Douglas/British Aerospace AV-8B Harrier II. Here one of six VMA-513 AV-8Cs deployed aboard USS *Tarawa* for Exercise Valiant Usher '86 hovers above the deck prior to transitioning to forward flight

Below The cramped cockpit and low profile canopy of the early Harrier illustrated here contrasts sharply with the big bubble hood of the new AV-8B

USS *Tarawa* underway with AV-8Cs, Bell AH-1T Sea Cobras, Boeing Vertol CH-46E Sea Knights and Sikorsky CH-53E Super Stallions ranged on deck. Can you spot the sole Bell UH-1N Huey?

Mission accomplished. A VMA-513 AV-8C pilot trudges to *Tarawa's* island for debriefing

When Valiant Usher '86 was over, tired but trusty old AV-8Cs went into storage at the Aerospace Maintenance and Regeneration Center (AMARC, formerly MASDC), Davis-Monthan AFB, Arizona, while VMA-513 got acquainted with their new AV-8Bs at MCAS Yuma

Fuelling time aboard *Tarawa*. A VMA-513 'brownshirt' checks the AV-8C's main landing gear, while a fellow crewman in combat fatigues and *Tarawa* sweatshirt finds a handhold on the Harrier's tailcone radar warning receivers

US Marine Corps helo pilots call their Boeing Vertol CH-46E Sea Knight twin-rotor helicopters 'Frogs'. A workhorse assault troop transport, a Frog can carry 18 combat-ready troops or 4200 lbs (1905 kg) of cargo at a maximum speed of 135 knots. These CH-46Es are from HMM-161 squadron, seen here aboard USS *Peleliu* in 1983

These pages and overleaf USMC CH-46Es
performing their routine but vital task of ferrying
men and supplies from USS *Tarawa* off the
coast of Western Australia during Exercise
Valiant Usher '86. Despite having only three
legs, the Sea Knight really does look like a
squatting Frog from some angles! USMC Sea
Knights are scheduled to be replaced by
Bell/Boeing Helicopter MV-22A Osprey tilt-rotor
craft commencing in December 1991

In bright, if not garish, contrast to the drab Field Green Frogs of the US Marine Corps, this US Navy HH-46A from Detachment Two of Helicopter Combat Support Squadron Five (HC-5) is a positive riot of colour. The star-spangled Sea Knight has just landed aboard the carrier USS *Enterprise* after a flight from its home ship USS *White Plains*. In addition to their routine stores replenishment duties, Sea Knights are the 'aerial mailmen' of the fleet, bringing welcome news from home for the 5000-plus crews of the supercarriers

Cargo culture. An HH-46A from HC-6 uplifts supplies for the USS *Coral Sea*. A crewman leans out of an open hatchway to check security and stability of the underslung load

Now in its 27th year of continuous service with the US Navy, the Sikorsky Sea King is a vital part of the Carrier Air Wing's anti-submarine warfare (ASW) armoury. These low visibility marked SH-3Hs recovering aboard the USS *John F Kennedy* are from HS-7 squadron. The red and yellow 'colander' device protruding from the starboard sponson is a magnetic anomaly detector (MAD) 'bird', which is reeled out behind the helicopter to seek variations in the Earth's magnetic field caused by the presence of a submarine

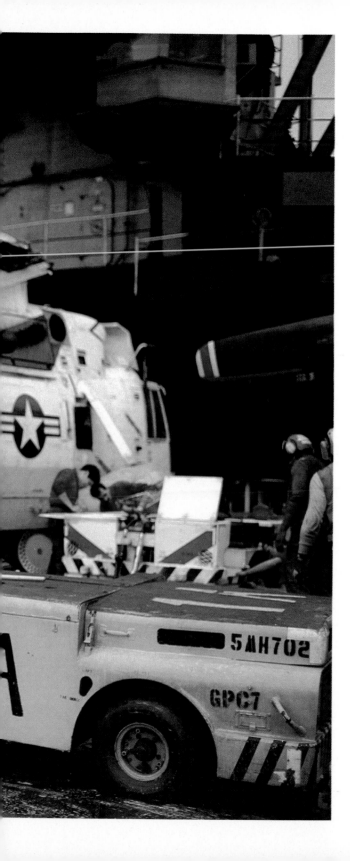

All folded and stowed, a high visibility (but grimy) light gull grey and white SH-3H from HS-17 shares the traditional helo parking spot in the shadow of *Coral Sea's* island with the ship's 'mule pool' of deck tractors

Main picture *Iwo Jima* class small assault carrier USS *Tripoli*, commissioned in 1966, is half the size of her *Tarawa* class cousins but plays an equally important role supporting US Marine Corps operations with the US Seventh Fleet

Inset Red eye special. With its seven-blade 79 foot (24.08 metre) diameter main rotor and entire tail section folded, this CH-53E Super Stallion of HMH-465 poses less of a parking problem aboard the USS *Tarawa* than you might expect from a helicopter capable of carrying 55 combat ready troops. Its three General Electric T64-GE-416 turboshaft engines total more than 13,000 shp, enabling the Sea Stallion to lift all but the very largest items of USMC combat equipment. Maximum fuel range of 1120 nm (2075 km) with the 1300 US gallon (4921 litre) drop tanks seen here outboard of each sponson is 1120 nm (2075 km), but can be extended by inflight refuelling from USMC Lockheed KC-130 tankers. The bulbous projection on the starboard side of the nose is the retractable inflight refuelling probe. CH-53Es have successfully conducted in-flight firing trials of AIM-9 Sidewinder missiles, which could be provided for self defence in combat situations

Above The (Royal) Navy's here! HMS *Illustrious*, second of the British *Invincible* class Light ASW carriers, sails into Freemantle Harbour, Australia during her Global '86 world cruise. Commissioned on 18 June 1982 for immediate service in the South Atlantic following the Falklands War, *Illustrious'* Sea Dart missile and 20 mm Mk 15 Vulcan Phalanx defensive systems are visible here. A Sea Harrier FRS.1 from 800 Naval Air Squadron is poised on the carrier's distinctive 'ski-jump', with Westland Sea King HAS.5s and AEW.2s lined up shipshape and Bristol fashion on deck

Top right *Illustrious'* 480-foot (146 metre) ski-jump ramp, here occupied by a brace of Sea Harriers, was the brilliant brainchild of Lieutenant Commander Doug Taylor, RN. It gives the Sea Harrier STOVL (Short Take Off and Vertical Landing) capability with full fuel and weapons loads irrespective of over-deck wind conditions. *Illustrious'* seven degree ramp (and sister ship *Invincible's*) will be refitted to 12 degrees to match that of *Ark Royal* by 1990

Right Sea Harrier side number 123 totes 190 gallon (864 litre) combat drop tanks and AIM-9L Sidewinder AAMs on underwing stores stations. 800 NAS's trident and crossed swords crest is displayed on the fin in the inevitable low-visibility style of the post-Falklands era